HEIRLOOM SEEDS

Preserving and Growing Organic Heirloom Vegetable Seeds

Amna Fadel

DISCLAIMER

Readers shall not transmit or reproduce any part of this book in any form including print, electronic, photocopying, scanning, mechanical, or recording without prior written permission from the author.

While the author has taken utmost efforts to ensure the accuracy of the written content, it is advisable for all readers to follow the information mentioned herein at their own risk. The author is not responsible for any personal or commercial damage caused by misinterpretation of information.

CONTENTS

INTRODUCTION

Photo by Steven Depolo / CC BY-SA 2.0

Have you ever heard farmers or agriculture professionals talking about saving seeds, or heirloom seeds or "brownbagging?" If you have, then you must have wondered what it is about, what it means, what kinds of seeds are heirloom seeds, and why would it means something important to people.

The fact is that over the past several hundreds of years, there are farmers and gardeners who have managed to maintain pure breeds of seeds for several hundreds of years. We live in a time where science has advanced largely and people have developed genetically enhanced seeds that produce more yield. However, while there are benefits of hybrid seeds, some people believe in preserving original seeds as well. Those who do that are saving seeds, or they are keepers of heirloom seeds.

You must be wondering how these heirloom keepers manage to preserve original forms of seeds, and whether you can do it too. You need to know that there is a lot involved in maintaining the purity of seeds. This is what you will discover upon reading this book. Therefore, if you want to become one of the few people in the world who strive towards preserving the natural nature of seeds, then this book will serve as a concise guide.

Continuing reading, and as you flip each page, you will master the art of seed saving.

UNDERSTANDING WHAT HEIRLOOM SEEDS ARE

An increasing number of people are becoming aware of heirloom vegetables, heirloom gardening and heirloom seeds. At the same time, most people are turning to or returning to traditional gardening methods for several reasons. One of the main reasons is an increasing interest in consuming healthy and natural foods, or food with the natural flavor they used to have while growing up. For others, the main reason is that they need a personal farm because purchasing food requires stretching the budget, and for some, the main reason is to indulge in a personal DIY challenge and exercise or outdoor activity.

There is no doubt that today; most hybrid seeds have lost the original flavor. Most seeds taste different and recipes of old hardly taste the same. Somehow, all this has led to some confusion about what heirloom seeds truly are. For some, the term simply means "organic." For others, an heirloom seed means something that is NOT GMO or GMS, i.e. not Genetically Modified Organism/Seeds. On the other hand, some people believe that GMO is good, and heirlooms are modified for improvement.

Let's look at some common definitions of "heirloom seeds" so that we can understand them better and compare them to GMS.

For some people, an heirloom means something of value that belongs to the family, a particular group of people or to a person, and it passes down from generations-to-generations. Ideally, an heirloom can be anything from jewels, to furniture to seeds. When a seed passes down generations, it becomes an heirloom seed.

For an heirloom seed, the value lies in the productivity, its flavor and its adaptability. According to ancient history, heirloom seeds date back to three hundred years, or even more. People have preserved only those seeds that have the best flavors, yield, that are dependable varieties and species that are rare to find. In fact, some heirlooms are very delicate species that are rare to find and hardly survive.

Another way of defining heirloom seeds that you will find in the world is the word "open-pollinated." However, they don't mean the same thing! An open pollinated seed is just a variety of seeds that come from a single variety, germinate, go into storage, and farmers replant them the following year and the cycle repeats. Open pollinations are why there is a variety of heirlooms existing today. Besides, most people are introducing new varieties, but obviously, you cannot mistake these varieties for original heirloom seeds.

Another term that you will hear is "organic certification." People get their crops certified through this process, by growing them under strict and uniform sets of standards. The process of certification involves inspections of the farm, processing facility, a detailed record keeping system, testing the water and soil to ensure that the people growing and handling the seeds comply with the standards set by the USDA (U.S. Department of Agriculture). Agencies like CCOF, OCAI, QAI, and Oregon Tilth ensure that the growers and harvesters comply with the standards. In short, according to some definitions, "heirlooms" mean "Organic" which means seeds grown by following certain standards.

However, you must not confuse heirloom seeds for "hybrid seeds." These are seeds produced artificially using techniques like cross-pollination, involving two genetically different plants that belong to the same species. Handlers ensure cross-pollination happens using the hand-technique, and the resulting seed will never be like either parent seeds. Therefore, the farmer will have no other choice but to purchase new seeds each year. The main purpose of hybrids is commercial use, and to make profits, using their characteristics like high yield, better tolerance for climatic changes, better resistance to diseases, uniformity in growth, better ripening, etc. Even the flavor varies.

Hybrids first began to appear from 1920-1930s, mostly in small localities where growers were willing to explore options for better yield. Generally, the GMO seeds were seeds with altered DNA, which made them completely different from the parent plants. The major crops that appeared as modified crops included corn, soybeans, wheat and cotton.

Heirlooms are special because of two distinct characteristics, which are excellent flavor and adaptability. Some varieties of heirlooms tomato seeds have become popular because they adapt to places within 2-3 harvests. At the same time, they show resistance to diseases.

Now that you understand what heirloom seeds are, and since you've cleared any misunderstanding you might have had, let us look at the history of heirloom seeds.

THE BRIEF HISTORY OF HEIRLOOM SEEDS

About 12,000 years ago, humanity began to change its approach to lifestyle and turned towards gathering livestock and more stable agriculture. People of that time settled down and started focusing on planting and cultivating food and domesticating animals for better living. This period was the Neolithic Revolution of human history.

Eventually, humanity began to choose seeds and saving them to plant them later, especially seeds of plants that showed better yield, tasted better, the ones that remained edible for a longer period and those that were capable of surviving harsh weather.

Several generations of the process of selective breeding led farmers of those times to achieve stable crops on which they could depend for sustenance for the entire community.

Although historians believe that the first signs of domestication of animals and plants first appeared in the Middle East, it seems more likely that it happened independently all over the world at almost the same period, roughly between 10,000-5,000 BCE. Each group that indulged in domestication began doing so through different plants. Here's a chart showing a summary of worldwide domestication of plants:

Location	Plant
Middle East	Wheat and Barley
Mesoamerica	Maize, Squash and Beans
South America	Potato
North America	Amaranth
China	Rice and Millet
Africa	Sorghum

Families began to pass these seeds down across generations and the seeds found their way into subsequent centuries. When people began to immigrate into the Americas, they brought their special seeds with them. In fact, these heirloom seeds were so precious that owners immigrating into Ellis Island used to have their heirloom seeds sewed into their clothing so that the authorities at Ellis Island could not confiscate them. To those people, these seeds meant survival in a harsh new world and they served as a reminder of their past.

When industrial revolution began, most farmers gave up on their farming and moved to bigger cities in search of a better life and a different lifestyle. Some of them did bring the seeds and plant them in their backyard gardens, and during World Wars, these seeds supplied them with a limited source of food. However, after the wars ended, backyard gardening faded away, but preservation of heirloom seeds continued. Perhaps the main reason for this was the emotional value and heritage owners of these seeds associated with the seeds. Although some times, heirlooms became hybrids with other species they never lost their value for developing inborn resistance to diseases, and remained very flavorful.

Later in the book, we will discuss what hybrids of heirloom exist and how they come about.

So, now that you know the history of heirloom seeds, the next time you come across vegetation that is heirloom seeds, make sure you willingly spend a dollar to enjoy rich flavor from ancient times. Now let's look at the sources of heirloom seeds so that you can know where to find them.

SOURCES OF HEIRLOOM SEEDS

Over the past several hundreds of years, as industrialization also influenced agriculture, people established companies dedicated to cultivating and preserving heirloom seeds. If you are looking for original, pure breed seeds, then you must look for such companies within or close to your location. With internet available, you can easily Google such information.

Some famous names in the world include:

- Seed Savers Exchange
- Organic Seed Alliance
- Kusa Seed Society
- High Mowing Organic Seeds
- Territorial Seed

WHY WOULD YOU SAVE SEEDS?

The main reasons for you to want to save seeds are because, you want to preserve their original characteristics like taste, nutritional value, disease resistant capability, and to pride yourself in being the owner of a pure. Moreover, they are ancient breeds of seeds in natural and original forms that go back to three hundred years, or maybe back to twelve thousand years ago.

Sometimes, saving seeds can even serve as an opportunity for you to make an exchange with other seeds that you need, without spending too much. Because heirloom seeds have so much economic importance, people are usually open to exchanging heirloom seeds for other seeds.

Besides, if you have just a few heirloom seeds, you can easily use them to grow more. Additionally, by planting heirloom seeds, you will be able to preserve the best ones that survived diseases and were resistant to bad weather. The next lot you cultivate will be even better adapted and will have a better yield. This means that you will be helping the world by producing better crops each year, and at the same time, you will save cost. Since there won't be diseases to fight and fewer losses, you will be looking at less expenses and higher profits.

Lastly, you would want to save heirloom seeds because you would not want to go for GMOs, open pollinated and hybrid seeds.

HOW YOU CAN GROW HEALTHY HEIRLOOM SEEDS

The first thing that you need before you can go ahead with growing your personal collection of heirloom seeds is to make sure that the seeds are healthy. You can make sure of this by looking out for some characteristics.

CHARACTERISTICS OF HEALTHY HEIRLOOM SEEDS

The characteristics of healthy heirloom seeds, under ideal conditions include:

1. Vigor – This refers to how vigorously the seeds grow into seedlings and how strong the seeds are.
2. Viability – This refers to the percentage of the batch that grows or germinates into seedlings
3. Maturity – This refers to making sure that the seeds have everything the seedlings need to grow into mature plants
4. Size – This is checking whether the seeds are large and have formed normally and completely

All of these characteristics affect one another. We cannot say that the characteristics stand independent of one another. All of these characteristics confirm whether the plant grows successfully under normal conditions. When we say "ideal conditions," we mean the right temperature, wind factor, availability of nutrients and water, sunlight, and air pressure.

It is a rule with heirloom seeds that healthy plants always make healthy seeds. If the plant is diseased, then the seeds will also have diseases, and the plant they sprout will have the disease the parent plant had. Therefore, the seeds that you choose to save must satisfy all the requirements, by showing the characteristics listed earlier.

WHY NOT SMALL SEEDS?

Choosing small seeds to save as heirloom seeds is a bad idea because small seeds save small amounts of food, which is insufficient for emerging seedlings. This leads to seedlings with poor health. Even if, in the presence of ideal conditions, the seedling begins to germinate, it may not have the strength to grow from the soil. Ultimately, it will either die, or grow as a weak plant. If you save such seeds, the next generations will continue to be weak. This goes against the concept of saving heirloom seeds.

STRESSING PLANTS DELIBERATELY TO FORCE ADAPTATION

Purposely stressing plants in their early lives helps to accelerate 'natural selection'. However, once the flowering stage approaches, remove the stresses as much as possible, this allows healthy seed formation and growth.

Stressing the plants further in extreme cases leads to a stage where even the ones that are well developed make starved seeds (smaller plants for faster results). In such a case, you should treat the seeds with more care during its planting and germination stage and replant them again every year, if not it will compromise their viability and vigor.

GET RID OF DISEASED PLANTS

If a parent plant is not healthy, it also affects the health of the seeds they yield over generations. This is a reason why it is important that you do not allow any diseased plant to produce any seed. Remove them from growing areas and dispose them off either by burning or hot composting so that only healthy seeds form.

EARLY FORMATION OF SEEDS

The initial stage of plant growth is important to the final viability of the seed. The plant during its early stages of development has to be healthy, strong and have minimal stress. At this stage, give the plants plenty of water, fertilizer and light, so that they grow strong and produce healthy flowers.

THE IMPORTANCE OF WATER IN SEED FORMATION

Water plays a particularly important role at the flowering stage, and pollen development stage of a plants growth. If you give too little water to the seed at the early stages, it leads to poor yield and can affect the vigor and health of your seedlings and seeds.

MATURATION OF SEEDS

Equally, dry conditions (warm between 80°F to 95°F) are also important to the final viability, vigor and storage of life of your seeds in the final stages. Excess watering of your mature seeds slows the natural process of their preparation for dormancy, extending the duration in which they use up the stored food reserves for respiration. In the end, this lowers the weight of the seed and affects their storage life as well.

Repeatedly drying and wetting of mature seeds not only delays dormancy markedly but also damages seeds due to alternate shrinking and swelling of the tissues in the seed. If they remain on the plant during rainy periods, then the seeds may also mold or form mildew in their husks or pods. Due to these reasons, it is best that you harvest seeds and bring them inside in the final drying stage so that they mature and remain dry (especially in rainy days).

BIENNIAL PLANTS AND OVER-WINTERING

Biennial plants like chard, collards, kale mature in the course of one year, and then they produce seeds early in the second year of their growth. In mild winter areas, collecting seeds from such plants is not a problem. However, in the cooler northern regions biennial plants need winter protection in order to survive and produce healthy seeds.

One way of assisting these plants in harsh conditions is by growing them in greenhouses, with the help of these, you can control their exposure to the freezing winter and help them properly mature. In case the plants freeze, you can apply thick mulch so that the plants survive in extreme winter.

'HEELING IN' BIENNIAL PLANTS

Another way of protecting biennial plants in harsh conditions is by digging them and 'heeling them in' over harsh winter in damp peat or sand. Biennial plants usually remain dormant over winter and by doing so; they remain safe during the cold months.

Ensure that you dig in plants with sufficient root ball, and remove small leaves and branched to keep the moisture loss to a minimum level. Then you can bury the plants in the moist peat or sand or other inert materials, exposing only the crown of the plants (Crowns are likely to rot if buried). Lastly, a plastic sheet tent will help in protecting the crowns from drying out during their storage stage.

When early spring approaches, temperatures likely stay above 28F, then remove the plants from their safe places and transfer them in containers. Then store these newly replanted ones in a protected area to allow them to harden off (allow them to adjust to outdoor environment) for a week or two before finally planting them in a proper garden.

TRUST YOUR EXPERIENCE

With all the information above, you should use your experience as the final ruling. Most Biennial plants do not survive the harsh conditions and if you live in such a region, you can make your own experience! Use different methods as experiments to decide the level of protection your plants will need to stay safe and grow healthy in such harsh weather conditions.

PRESERVING HEIRLOOM SEEDS

Depending on your reason for preserving or saving heirloom seeds, you approach will vary. Therefore, the first thing that you have to do is decide on what you want. Do you want to…?

    a.   Create new varieties that are better adapted to your gardening taste and style

    b.   Preserve the genetic makeup of the variety you have

In this chapter, we will discuss how you can preserve the heirloom seeds and maintain their genetic constitution. You need to bear in mind that preservation is very different from cultivating your personal garden and maintaining it in different climates, or in different habitats. The chances that you will succeed with preserving the heirloom seeds are quite great and definitely worth the try. You just need to take into account the different factors that will influence the harvest and purity of your seeds.

For instance, you have to make sure that the chances of cross breeds with other species in as low as zero. You can make sure of this by first getting rid of any other species nearby because wind, insects and your hands can mistakenly pick pollens and drop them into the flower's reproductive system. Assess the wind and insect transmission factor carefully. After that, follow these five simple steps to preserve you heirloom seeds:

STEP #1: Allow the seeds of the plant to form. Do not remove the flowers and do not reap the fruits immediately they ripen. Instead, you have to let the flowers to die naturally, and then allow the fruits or vegetables to become overripe.

STEP #2: Let the seeds dry completely. There will be visible changes in color, like in vegetables the pod turns to yellow or brown while drying. Corn seedpods develop a hard exterior and tend to shrivel as they dry. Flowers lose their petals and their stem turns brown from green.

STEP #3: Pluck off the seeds from the seedpods using your fingers and snip the seeds off carefully. You may want to use a clean set of scissors for this.

STEP #4: Let the pods dry. You can do this by laying them on a newspaper and placing them in a warm and dry location. You should allow the pods to dry for at least 1-2 weeks.

STEP #5: Remove the shell of the pods. When the pods dry, they become easy to peal because they crumble. This protects the insides of the seeds, and you get undamaged heirloom seeds.

STEP #6: Either use them right away, or save them somewhere where they will remain safe until you need them.

If you choose to breed the seeds, then you need to do what the next chapter says. Continue reading…

YOU CAN BREED YOUR OWN VARIETY

This is the best part about heirloom seeds – you can create your own variety! The breed you create can adapt to the environmental conditions that you want. Here is what you need to do first; select the new strain that you want from the existing heirloom seeds variety.

For this, you need to allow the plant to grow and display all its amazing qualities. Then you will be able to decide what characteristics you want to capitalize on. Good candidates will have characteristics like better yield, high tolerance to draught, disease resistance. You must weigh the advantages and disadvantages of choosing the variety before you proceed with breeding. For that, here is what you need to do:

ASSESS ADVANTAGES AND DISADVANTAGES OF SEED SELECTION

You must pay attention to the advantages and disadvantages that the particular plant offers. Check its genetic health and the diversity it offers. Make sure it has better qualities than the previous generation before you select it.

If there are disadvantages of the plant, like being too susceptible to diseases and being sensitive to bad weather, it will be a disadvantage to choose it.

SELF-SELECTION LOWERS GENETIC DIVERSITY

It's a scientific rule – plants that self-select themselves tend to lose their genetic material. If you do not counteract this loss, then the selected variety will have a smaller and less varied gene pool than an original variety does. When we say "gene pool," we are referring to the sum total of all the genetic traits in the entire population. A single plant cannot contain all the genes available in the entire variety of the plant.

Genetic narrowing will include genes that give the plant useful qualities under different growing conditions. However, the plants in your newly selected variety may not have the genetic ability to grow or survive to a wide range to conditions as its parent plant did in the last generation, even though it may show signs of better growth in a particular season.

Why the gene pool may be smaller is because the new variety forms by subtracting the new traits from the old ones. This is why; farmers plant only a few of the seeds from an original variety with the new variety so that they can prevent genetic loss.

MAINTAIN GENETIC DIVERSITY

Keeping genetic narrowing in mind, do not start with planting an already well-refined variety of seeds. That's because in the previous selection, there is a high possibility that the plant might have lost useful traits that can help it grow in the present conditions. Therefore, it is highly recommendable that you begin with diversifying.

USE A DIVERSE VARIETY

Using an older and more variety of seeds will offer you a broader and potentially useful range of characteristics to select. A wide initial variation gives you better chances of finding the type of adaptations that you are looking for in the new generation, and at the same time provides more genetic variations to work with.

MIX FAVORITES FOR WIDER GENETIC BASE

You can also prevent genetic narrowing by growing two or more seed varieties together for the next two years. After that, select your new seeds from the resulting new seeds.

ADVANTAGES OF ASSORTMENT

When you select particular seeds, or make an assortment of your own choice of seeds, you can maintain consistence in the traits that you value most. For example, good taste, better flowers, prettier foliage, improved adaptation to the climate and physical conditions, etc. When you select individual plants in a variety that has good traits and is better than others are, and discard those that are less adapted or improved, you end up creating more of the useful variety.

Note however, that discarding seeds is not recommendable because then you can lose the genetic constitution of the original seeds completely.

DIFFERENCE BETWEEN SELECTION AND PRESERVATION

There is a clear difference between the words "Selection" and "Preservation."

Selection means choosing the best seeds and storing them.

Preservation means using methods to store the selected seeds.

You must not confuse yourself about these two words. If you want to, you can actually practice both selection and preservation. All you need to do is treat both batches of seeds separately. We will come to more on this later when we talk about avoiding unconscious selection and cross-pollination.

MAKING BREEDING SELECTIONS

The first thing that you can do is to plant a variety as usual, and then select the traits you want. Start with a large plantation so that you can increase the chances of finding plants that have all the traits that you are looking for. It's as easy as that!

If you are selecting more than one distinct trait, then you can maintain the best results from the newly selected isolated seeds in the next planting. This will allow the traits to stabilize without cross-pollination. Make sure that you remove all unwanted seeds before planting; otherwise, you will risk preserving the traits you achieved.

HYBRIDIZING AND STABILIZATION

While cross-pollination is something you must avoid, hybrid crossing is not entirely a taboo. When you allow different heirloom seeds to cross-pollinate or hybridize, the yield will have a more diverse genetic pool of the traits you wanted. Then you can regrow the variety, select the best ones, and stabilize them to true-to-type breeds.

Once again, never hybridize rare heirloom seeds that you need to preserve. Use those seeds that have plentiful sources and that you know you can discard if you don't need the traits.

CREATE OPEN-POLLINATED PLANTS USING HYBRIDS

To create open-pollinated plants using hybrids, use two or more varieties and regrow the resulting crossed seeds. Regrow them until the traits you want stabilize and that's it! You've created a new open-pollinated variety!

To create hybrid plants, you need to use various methods that may vary from simple to complex.

A simple method is to grow the seeds normally in close proximity, and allow natural cross-pollination. The first generation will have mixed characteristics, then you can allow them to continue mixing and stabilizing on their own, or you can separate them into groups that have particular traits in common and allow these to cross.

The other method is to use hybrid seeds and stabilizing them by planting your favorite varieties and letting them produce seeds. Then you can collect the seeds and replant them over several generations, and each time select seeds from the plants that show the traits that you seek, and then allowing the plants to cross-pollinate on their own, naturally. This way, you can easily have stabilized new seeds, and a variety of open-pollinated seeds. Soon, you will not have to rely on the original hybrid variety.

CREATING AND STABILIZING YOUR "F2" HYBRIDS

Talking in technical terminologies, "F1" refers to a conventional hybrid. You can produce such a plant by hand-pollination, using a female and male of different varieties. You can even use plants of two different but close species. Then, allow the female to produce the seeds and keep crossing the seeds with that of any other plant. Through this controlled method, you will create very specific, hybrid plant with high yield trait. This is your F2 hybrid!

You will have to use varying levels of care. Each F1 hybrid will contain extreme genetic diversity.

Then, you can use F1 offspring seeds of one generation to mix them with another generation, creating the F2 generation. Unlike the F1 generation, the F2 generation will show a wider range of physical traits that offer better advantage; however, they will not be stable. This is why; F2 seeds do not produce true-to-type offspring seeds.

SIGNIFICANCE OF HEIRLOOM SEEDS

The main importance of heirloom seeds is their true purpose. That is;

- Preserving the original genetic constitution of the species
- Preserving their original traits that existed thousands of years ago
- Offering users a chance to select and isolate the traits that they find beneficial
- Offering users a chance to improve the quality and quantity of their yield
- In economically challenging situations, selling heirloom seeds can bring you some extra income

Therefore, you must appreciate their significance.

WHAT ARE ORIGINAL HEIRLOOM PLANTS?

Original heirlooms are simply seeds of plants that people grew thousands of years ago. They passed on seeds with the best qualities to the following generations as the most valuable possessions. Humanity found them as a way of preserving the best and original taste, and other qualities of plants.

In other words, they are seeds of plants that are not "open-pollinated" or "hybrids." Let's discuss what these two are in more details.

THE DIFFERENCE BETWEEN OPEN-POLLINATED AND HYBRID SEEDS

Although people make a big deal about the difference between open-pollinated and hybrid seeds, there really isn't too much to it. It is simple to understand.

OPEN-POLLINATED SEEDS

'Open-pollinated' is just another term that people use for heirloom seeds interchangeably. However, they don't mean the same thing. An open-pollinated seed is a variety that people can plant, save for several years, replant them and the same variety will grow year-after-year.

We can say that all heirloom seeds are open-pollinated seeds, but we cannot say that all open-pollinated seeds are heirloom seeds. That's because now there is a huge variety of open-pollinated seeds but their characteristics are not good enough to make them heirlooms.

HYBRID SEEDS

Hybrid seeds are the result of artificial pollination between two genetically different plants, but of the same species. For example, you can create hybrids using tomatoes of different species, or corn of two species. In this case, you can induce cross-pollination by hand. The offspring will not be entirely like either parent, which is why each year, you will have to buy new seeds to grow the parent species.

BENEFITS OF OPEN- POLLINATED SEEDS AND HYBRID SEEDS

The benefits of using open-pollinated or/and hybrid seeds are that, first, you can save the seeds each year and you will not have to buy new seeds for every season. In the case of hybrids, they are mostly cross-pollinated plants that produce better and more resistant plant varieties. Besides, since most open-pollinated plants have come from hybrids or cross-pollinated plants, they have the same benefits to offer as hybrids do. When people plant hybrids and open-pollinated seeds, there is guarantee that at least two out of ten plants will be true to the parent plants. If farmers can plant these seeds for seven years, they will get a generation that is true to the parent plants. Therefore, you never really lost the original genetic constitution of any species.

WHAT IS THE DIFFERENCE BETWEEN ANGIOSPERMS AND GYMNOSPERMS

Just as humans and animals have different characteristic features, plants also have some significant differences. To make it easier for people to understand the difference between the types of plants you find, there are two broad groups of plants: Angiosperms and Gymnosperms. Here is a chart to explain the differences between them:

	Angiosperms	Gymnosperms
Definition	These are seed-producing flowering plants. They have seeds enclosed within an ovary	These are seed-producing non-flowering plants. They have "naked" seeds that are not enclosed
Seeds	Enclosed in an ovary, this is usually the fruit	The seeds are bare, usually found on the leaves, cones and scales
Lifecycle	They are seasonal plants (usually die during fall or autumn)	These are evergreen plants
Tissue	Triploid (triple fusion produces endosperms)	Haploid (production of endosperm happens before fertilization)
Reproduction	Via flowers. Unisexual	Via cones.

	or bisexual	Unisexual
Leaves	Flat	Needle-like or scale-like
Cotyledon	Present; may be single (monocotyledonous) or in pairs (dicotyledonous)	Absent
Wood	Hardwood	Softwood
Periniality	Non-perennial	Perennial
Pollination	Rely on a medium (animals or hand)	Rely on wind
Uses	Medicines, clothing, food, etc.	Lumber, paper, furniture, etc.

This will help you understand what kinds of heirloom plants you can work with. The next thing that you need to know about is how these heirloom plants germinate.

UNDERSTANDING THE PROCESS OF GERMINATION

By definition, the process of germination leads to the growth of a plant from a seed. When you plant a seed in the soil, a lot happens. After several processes, the seedling finally sprouts and the plant that comes from the seed will be an angiosperm or a gymnosperm.

THE PROCESS OF GERMINATION

For germination to happen properly, there are certain conditions required. The seed must have optimum temperature, water and oxygen supply in the soil. This is why; you cannot plant the seed too deep under the soil, and you cannot over flood the water, and you cannot plant the seed under extreme temperature conditions. You have to make sure that there is just enough light and not too much heat, otherwise the germination process will end and the plant dies.

There are three stages of germination:

Stage 1: When the seedling gets water supply, there is imbibition, its outer seed coat ruptures, and it needs optimum temperature for metabolic and enzyme activities to happen that will lead to the formation of a seedling.

Stage 2: Imbibition of the seed coat leads to the emergence of the plumule and the radicle, and the cotyledon unfolds. At this point, optimum temperature and light exposure are important.

Stage 3: This is the final stage when the cotyledons expand to form the leaves.

For germination to happen smoothly, the seed needs food, water and light. Food substances include proteins, fats, and carbohydrates, which are usually stored inside the cotyledons.

Hormones like auxins and heteroauxins control the growth of the plants and the development of seeds.

FACTORS REQUIRED FOR GERMINATION

The main factors required for proper germination are:

1. Water
2. Optimum temperatures
3. Light
4. Fertilizer (later on)

INTERNAL FACTORS

Internal factors refer to the hormones that promote growth and provision of food stored inside the cotyledon. If the seed is defective and the cotyledon doesn't provide enough food, the seedling will not grow well and may even die. As the plant grows, you will have to use fertilizers to compensate its needs.

EXTERNAL FACTORS

External factors refer to physical environmental factors that influence the seed's growth. These include temperature, pressure, water, wind, sunlight.

HOW TO HARVEST AND CLEAN YOUR SEEDS

There are two main categories of harvesting and cleaning seeds, and these depend on whether the harvest is fruits or seeds, and whether if they are dry or wet when they mature. As soon as you see that the fruit or the plant has completely formed and is starting to show signs of ripening, it is time to harvest them.

In some fruits and vegetables, the color of the fruit or vegetable can tell whether it is ready for harvest or not. In tomatoes for instance, while they are green or greenish-yellow, they are not ready for harvest. In corn, you cannot peel off the cover but you can feel it to know if the corn seeds are ready and hard enough for harvest.

CLEANING DRY SEEDS

These include seeds like beans, peppers, okra, basil, carrots and onions, and plants that belong to these families. Cleaning the dry seeds involves letting it dry enough to let the pods and husk crumble, and then you can separate the seeds from the chaff by screening and winnowing it.

Winnowing it means dropping the seeds or chaff mixture from a height from one container into another in the direction of the wind and letting it separate the husk from the seeds.

CLEANING WET SEEDS

You can find wet seeds in fruity or pulpy plants like tomatoes, squashes and eggplants. To clean these, you need to wash the seeds and separate them from the pulp and wash them in clean water. The good seeds will sink to the bottom in the container while the bad seeds and pulp will float. Then, spread the seeds on a cloth or ceramic container, and let them dry in mild sunlight. If you leave them wet for seven days, they will rot or ferment.

HOW TO KEEP THEM PURE

The easiest way for you to keep your heirloom plants pure is by preventing them from crossbreeding. For this, you don't need any special skills or special knowledge. However, what you need is a fair idea about how close is too close to plant the seeds. Make sure that you plant the seeds at enough distance from one another to prevent cross-pollination. Yes, insects might do their work, but if you can keep insects away, and keep wind speed in mind, and then space the plants far enough, you can prevent cross-pollinations.

METHOD OF MINIMIZING CROSS-POLLINATION

When you have dried and cleaned the seeds, make sure that you keep each plant's seeds separate. Do not mix the seeds of different seeds together, because when planting, you might make the wrong crops grow next to each other and risk the purity of your heirloom seeds.

Let us look at some methods that you can implement to make sure that you minimize cross-pollination.

DISTANCE ISOLATION PLANTING

When professional farmers say that they use "distance Isolation planting techniques" to preserve their heirloom seeds, what are they trying to say? It simply means using distance between the plants to prevent them from having any form of cross-pollination.

As we have discussed so far, plants can have cross-pollination or open-pollination to create offspring seeds. If you want to preserve the purity of your heirloom seeds, then your greatest challenge is to prevent these from happening on their own. When you plant the seeds at particular distances, you are minimizing the risk of their pollens from dropping onto the female reproductive organ (ovary) by air, insects and hand transfer.

If you are wondering what distance is ideal to make sure the risk of cross-pollination is minimal, then the best advice you can have is to follow the distance that the USDA recommends.

DISTANCE ISOLATION AND SELF-POLLINATION

Even if you keep a gap of at least 2 miles between two species that you cultivate, there is always a chance that the heirloom plants will undergo self-pollination. This happens in plants with both male and female reproductive organs. Such plants are what we know as "Self-pollinators."

You need to protect self-pollinators who pollinate themselves immediately their flowers open. For example, Okra and peppers can fertilize themselves. You can use cages to prevent them from self-pollinating.

However, some self-pollinating plants fertilize themselves even before their flowers open, for example, tomatoes and beans. They are exclusive self-pollinators. Plants that don't self-pollinate naturally have better chances of preservation when farmers implement techniques to protect them from cross-pollination.

DISTANCE ISOLATION AND PREVENTION OF WIND POLLINATION

For plants that flower, the chances of cross-pollination is high due to wind pollination. When you plant such plants at a distance, it minimizes the chances of cross-pollination largely. Depending on how light the pollens of the male plant are, the distance they can travel in the wind varies. You will have to keep this in mind while planting using distance isolation. Plan the distance wisely because the distances needed to prevent wind pollination varies with the environmental conditions in your location. You have to consider factors like wind patterns, windbreaks that exist, wind strength and others. Windbreaks are effective for plants that have heavy pollens, like corn. Wind pollinated plants that grow in woody areas with low wind need less distance than plants that grow in open, vast and windy areas.

ISOLATION OF GENETICALLY PURE SEEDS

If you decide to grow more than one crossable variety at a time, and you still want to keep the seeds genetically pure, what you need to do is isolate the heirloom varieties from one another. Make sure that they don't mix through cross-pollination. If you fail, then the offspring will be a hybrid. Apart from distance isolation, you can use screened cages, cover individual flowers with bags, or time the plantation so that the two or more varieties never flower at the same time.

USING TIMED ISOLATION

If you cannot use distance isolation because you have limited space to cultivate, and caging is too costly or problematic for you, then you can use time isolation. This technique allows you to work with two varieties that shed their pollen within a limited period, and mature at different times. This will make sure that neither plant is receptive of the pollens because while one matures the other will already be past the stage of reproduction.

Suppose that the flowering periods of the two crossable plants overlaps slightly, you can still use time isolation to prevent cross-pollination. The trick here is to remove those plants that will flower late manually. Remove flower buds long before they open.

CAGING TO AVOID WIND POLLINATION

If you have to use caging because distance isolation is not an option for you, then you need to know that it is a great technique. You can easily use it to preserve your heirlooms. If you cannot buy cages, then you can buy bags. Put bags over individual flowers to prevent their pollens from moving to flowers of other plants. This will prevent wind-pollination and cross-pollination.

CAGING TO PREVENT INSECT POLLINATION

Apart from preventing wind and cross pollination, caging and bagging will also prevent insect pollination. You can use large frames of window screens to hold the mesh a little away from the plants inside the cage. This will prevent insects from getting to the flowers. Make sure that the cage that you build is large enough to accommodate the plants when they mature. As soon as they start flowering, place the cage over the plants. Remove flowers that mature too soon to prevent insect pollination before you place the cages.

The use of caging procedures varies with whether the plants you are working with can self-pollinate or require insect-pollination. If they are insect-dependent for pollination, then you can use the "alternate day caging" technique.

USING THE ALTERNATE DAY CAGING METHOD

This technique involves your removing the cage periodically, so that insects can periodically reach the flowers and pollinate them. This is for insect-dependent plants in particular. You have to work with two or three varieties, cover them with separate cages and remove the cage for only one variety every two to three days. Do not remove the cage from the other two varieties; otherwise, there will be hybrid crossing, and you will lose the purity of your heirlooms.

For self-pollinated plants that are also insect-pollinated, you can leave them in the cage full time, and they will still produce seeds.

POLLINATION BY HAND AND BAGGING

If you don't want to use any of the techniques above, or if you want to have high control over the plant pollination in your farm, then you can always use hand pollination to pollinate them, and then close them in paper bags. This technique is ideal for plants with large flowers like daylilies and squash.

DISTANCES FOR SEED ISOLATION

Here is a table with USDA recommended distances that you can use for each variety.

Plant	USDA Isolation Distance	Pollinator
Amaranth	None specified	Wind, Insect
Arugula	660 feet[7]	Insects
Basil	None specified	Insects
Common Bean	None specified	Self
Fava Bean	None specified	Self
Lima Bean	None specified	Self
Tepary Bean	Not specified	Self
Beet	Not specified	Wind
Broccoli	660 feet	Insects
Broomcorn	660 feet	Self
Brussels Sprouts	660 feet	Insects
Cabbage	660 feet	Insects
Cantaloupe	¼ miles	Insects

Carrot	Not specified	Insects
Cauliflower	660 feet	Insects
Celery	Not specified	Insects
Chinese cabbage	660 feet	Insects
Chinese Mustard	660 feet	Insects
Chives	¼ miles	Insects
Collards	660 feet	Insects
Cilantro	Not specified	Insects
Corn	660 feet	Wind
Cotton	¼ miles	Self, Insects
Cowpea	0	Self
Cucumber	¼ miles	Insects
Dill	Not specified	Insects
Eggplant	Not specified	Self
Fennel	Not specified	Insect
Garlic	¼ miles	Insect
Garlic Chives	¼ miles	Insect
Gourds	¼ miles	Insect
Kale	660 feet	Insect
Lamb's Quarters	Not specified	Wind
Lettuce	Not specified	Self
Melon, Honeydew	¼ miles	Insects
Melon, Musk	¼ miles	Insects
Mustard	660 feet	Insects
Okra	825 feet	Self, Insect

Onion	¼ mile	Insect
Parsley	Not specified	Insect
Pea	0	Self
Pepper	30 feet	Self, Insect
Potato	30 feet	Self, Insect
Pumpkin	¼ mile	Insect
Radish	660 feet	Insect
Sorghum	Not specified	Self
Spinach	Not specified	Wind
Squash	¼ mile	Insect
Sunflower	½ mile	Insect
Swiss Chard	Not specified	Wind
Tomatillo	30 feet	Self
Tomato	30 feet	Self
Turnip	660 feet	Insect
Watermelon	¼ mile	Insect

Note: Those that are "not specified" vary with the location of the planter and varying environmental factors. Of course, with experience, you will be able to decide what distance works best for you.

The next thing that we need to discuss is how you can store these heirloom seeds for several years.

HEIRLOOM SEEDS STORING TIPS

This is one of the most important aspects of saving seeds. You have to prepare to store your special seeds and make sure that they remain preserved for several months without decaying. Then, when you decide to cultivate them, they should be as fresh as ever.

It is important to prepare the seeds for storage, and for this, you need to dry them, and keep them in proper conditions so that their chances to germinate well and produce healthy plants remain high. You can easily achieve this once you know their requirements.

DESICCATION INTOLERANT SEEDS

Some seeds cannot survive when they lose their water content, which means that drying them will result in losing the seeds completely, these are desiccation-intolerant seeds. However, most seeds are desiccation-tolerant. Therefore, before you start drying the seeds for storage purpose, make sure that they are desiccation-tolerant.

STORING DESICCATION-INTOLERANT SEEDS

After maturing, desiccation-intolerant seeds don't enter dormancy. Other processes like respiration and physiological changes continue, which cause such seeds to depreciate too quickly after they mature. This is why; farmers must plant them while they are fresh. If you dry such seeds, they will inevitably lose their viability and die, which means that you will lose your heirlooms.

Citrus seeds are "borderline desiccation-intolerant" seeds. They lose viability too quickly, but can germinate slowly after drying. This makes borderline desiccation-intolerant seeds to become damp and vulnerable to microbial damage in the germination stage. This means it is highly recommendable that you plant such seeds while they are fresh.

PREPARING FOR TEMPORARY STORAGE

Since these seeds cannot survive drying, you can store them for only a short time. For this, you have to keep the seeds moist and in cool temperatures (but do not freeze them). The moisture lets the seeds to respire, and the cool temperature prevents bacterial and fungal activities, and disallows rotting while they are in storage.

Here's what you have to do for preparing for storage for desiccation-intolerant seeds. Put them in a vessel with sufficient moist peat moss, and some paper towels or sand to prevent them from becoming too dry. Make sure that the lid is not completely closed, or make some holes in the lid to allow air to get into the container. Keep this container in a refrigerator, and make sure you use them soon enough.

STORING DESICCATION-TOLERANT SEEDS

When desiccation-tolerant seeds ripen and dry, they slow or almost cease their physiological processes. They get their food supplies by changing food reserves like starch and stable fats to sugars. In fact, some of these seeds require drying so that they can complete their ripening stage and go into dormancy until they have to germinate later in suitable conditions.

PREPARING FOR TEMPORARY STORAGE

The process of drying has to be slow and methodical, and then you must use desiccants if you are drying them in air that has more than 30% humidity. When you keep them in storage, you have to keep them at suitable temperature, and you must maintain moisture levels to ensure longevity.

Dry them properly by spreading them in a shady spot, where it is airy. In an air-conditioned environment, with humidity between 20-40% or more will be important. It will take two or more weeks to dry the seeds well enough. If the seeds are large, then it may take them longer to dry.

STORING AND RE-GROWING HEIRLOOM SEEDS

Even if you can maintain ideal conditions in storage, long-term or longstanding storage reduces the viability largely. As the length of storage time increases, the percentage of damage to the seeds due to tissue degeneration and mutations also increases. The roots particularly suffer in longstanding storage. Therefore, the more regularly you regrow the heirloom seeds, the better the plant's overall health will be. To test if they are dry enough before putting them into storage, use a hammer to hit them. If they bend, they are not dry enough, but if they crush completely, then they are dry enough.

SILICA GEL FOR ABSOLUTE DRYING

Seeds that you air-dry will need something extra like silica gel to ensure absolute drying before storage can happen, but you cannot use heat! You can dry them to maintain five to seven percent moisture content (by mass) and then you can store them in temperatures below freezing point. You can retain their viability for several years like this. Moreover, this method minimizes risk of mutation, which happens at higher temperatures and higher moisture content.

The quantity of silica gel that you use should be of equal weight as the seeds and keep them in a jar with proper sealing lid for seven to eight days. After that, move the thoroughly dried seeds to an airtight jar and place it in your freezer or refrigerator or keep it in a cool and dark place. Make sure that you read the instructions on the silica gel package carefully, otherwise a risk of your burning the seeds.

PROBLEMS TO AVOID WHILE STORING SEEDS

Even if you have prepared your seeds for storage, you need to be aware of some problems, and these are:

1. MOLD AND MILDEW

Mold and mildew arise due to incomplete drying. This means that you must ensure that they dry thoroughly, though not to zero percent moisture. You should lookout for sweating while the seeds are in a jar. If they sweat, it means there is too much moisture and you need to dry them further. Using desiccants at this point is a recommendation.

2. FLUCTUATING TEMPERATURE AND MOISTURE

When there is fluctuation in the moisture level or temperature, it reduces the seeds' longevity, making them more vulnerable to rot and death. High temperature and moisture fluctuations can lead to mutations on the root tips and affect the seed tissue.

Moreover, cellular mutations can occur, which affect the seed's metabolism and can cause failed germination.

Therefore, when you want to plant the seeds, bring them out of the cool place and let the container reach room temperature gradually. Do not open the seal of the container until it reaches room temperature. This is important, because you don't want moisture to condense on the seeds when you bring them out of storage.

3. INSECTS

Weevils and other insects can be a major threat to your heirloom seeds. You cannot ignore the possibility that these seeds are present in any seed collection. While seeds are frozen, they are safe from insect damage because although some insects are unavoidable, freezing temperatures can make the insects inactive or even kill them. Nevertheless, you need to guard your heirloom seeds against insect infestation.

To protect the seeds against insects, you can use diatomaceous earth (D.E.). Just add enough of the D.E into the jar to cover the surface of the seeds; gently stir it in to cover the seeds thoroughly. This is a wise non-toxic, inexpensive and safe way of preserving the seeds against insect attack.

ALL SET TO START SAVING HEIRLOOM SEEDS

Finally, you are at the point where you know everything about heirloom seeds, and you are all set to apply this knowledge. Now you know what heirloom seeds are and why people save them. You understand how to grow them on your own, and you know the characteristics of heirloom seeds so that you can differentiate them from usual seeds. You don't need an expert to tell you when you find a fake heirloom.

You also know how to preserve them, so you can work with a variety of heirloom seeds and grow a variety of the breeds. You understand their economic significance and you know why people guard them with too much care and affection.

The next time you hear people talk about open-pollinated and hybrid seeds, you will know what they are discussing. In addition, you've also learnt what are angiosperm and gymnosperms. The explanation on the process of germination in this book will serve as a guide for you, even if you want to cultivate non-heirloom seeds at any point in time. You also know the factors that can affect the process of germination, so you can control the conditions necessary for optimal growth.

When it is time to harvest, make sure you don't damage the heirloom seeds, and make sure that you preserve them as discussed in this book.

As a seed saver, your priority has to be minimizing the risk of unwanted cross-pollination so that you can preserve the purity of the heirloom's genetic constitution. We have discussed various methods that you can apply, like caging and bagging, and distance isolation technique.

When it comes to storage of heirloom seeds, you must make sure that you handle them with caution. Not all seeds can be in storage for too long, and we have discussed why this is so. Some seeds tend to retain moisture while others die when they are dry for too long. Be careful and use the right technique for the seeds. If you don't manage them well, the seeds will rot while they are in storage.

Apart from the temperature and moisture problem during storage, insect infestation is also a major storage problem about which you have to be careful. We have discussed this as well and you know what you need to do – use D.E.

Now, if you are interested in saving seeds, feel free to embark on this mission. It is not impossible to maintain a pure breed of heirloom seeds. Have fun, and save pure original seeds. You never know what the future hold and someday, perhaps in the next hundred years from now, the generation of people that exists can look back and thank you for saving original seeds.

www.ingramcontent.com/pod-product-compliance
Lightning Source LLC
Chambersburg PA
CBHW030538290526
45786CB00004B/1765